C000083847

A COSMIC GIRL'S DIARY

This book is a collection of absurd poetry about a woman's geometry.

Poetry must have been invented on a rainy day.

Dreams are practice of imagination,
Serving as bookmarks for
The ever-changing tides of time.
Indulge!

*

The splendour of chaos
The madness of silence
The loudness of stillness
The wriggle of now.

*

It is the need for love that puts a measure of equality
between all beings on this mighty Earth.

There is a great deal of ache in our world,
But without it,
All our hearts would be like unturned stones -
Plain COLD.

*

There is no secret to finding balance;
It's all about embracing the ebb and flow of life's
waves.

*

Only what matters comes your way -
Like the short summer rain
That falls from a sky that
Has travelled to see
The same ever changing souls.

Your skin - a pattern for my illusion,
My skin - an aroma inviting your intrusion.
We lay in the tall wet grass,
With our fingers combed together;
The wind translates our thoughts into the dark,
While we listen to the music of the gods.
Our eyes are blindly avoiding the light -
We are moths.
We seek salvation in the dark,
And we come together as one
To push open the gate to the stars.
The gate opens,
And we are back in our bed,
Staring at the sky,
Touching our wings -
We can finally fly.

Lost and forgotten,
Abandoned on a mobile phone that had run out of
fashion;
Lost and forgotten,
Somewhere in a house in Streatham Hill,
Across from an elementary school,
Where shouts, laughters and dreams
Are loudly knocking on windows,
Like sparrow's wings
Battling their own reflection.
Lost and forgotten,
Dozens of poems that I did not protect.

*

Ten minutes of white -
An echo bounces off the wall…
Walls here grow so tall
That they bear no ceiling but
The mighty sky in
Mid-afternoon glorious glow.
A voice creepy crawls
Into the mind - feverish
With memories of an attack
Of fears and anxious thoughts.
Day five. (Lockdown)

You wear that hat,
To shelter or to trap,
All those true or false memories that
you have.
Your denim shirt,
A shield to armour your heart -
Protection from any other music
That is not the poetry
You wrote and read;
Your poetry penetrates my every thought,
For a whole cosmic second.
Success has its regard.

*

It feels like these walls have eaten me so many times
before.
It feels like they've just spat me out.
I am covered in a clay of yesterday.
Where is the rain to wash it off?

Love thyself! Everyone else is taken! (Valentine's)

*

What is expected of your dreams after you have given
in to nightmares?
They transform into crystallised drops of light that
stare at you,
From a memory that crashed on Earth -
Forbidden and forgotten.
That is what dreams are: memories of pre humanity.

*

A lonely day will feel like it will never find its pair and
yet, it is a day mirrored by an infinite of other lonely
days.

The shadow of She who jumps with time -
A brand new concept of temptation,
That dances to ancestral rhymes;
It chants and faints and tries to lose
The Heaven that was trapped within her
And the Hell;
But it fails to break the eternal spell.

She chants again and thinks of
The dry mandrake leafs,
Hidden in between white starched sheets,
Reminiscent of her fear of the beast,
That ruled the mountains and the fields.

(Romanian Folklore)

Avoiding all certitude -
Sacrificing scientific explanation
For the sake of mystic exploration -
That is the animal within;
Creature of this land that
Interconnects us all through dreams,
That make sense in a material world,
Populated by recurring spirits.

*

It will be a white night:
Sleepless - bathing in moonlight,
And in so much snow delight.

(First snow of the year)

If a hug is long enough, nobody can resist it.

*

Why don't we send letters any more?
The act of sending a letter on a piece of paper had the
ability to carry not only the written words, but also the
essence of the sender. The scent of the sender, their
energy at the moment of writing, and even the sweat of
their efforts in folding the paper - all became
intertwined with the letter itself. In a sense, a letter
carried a unique DNA -like imprint of the sender,
making it a truly personal and meaningful form of
communication.

Standing in that corner,
Like a pillar of protection -
Unseen, unknown, invisible to the normal eye.
The air, cold and static
Smells of nothing and
Possesses the room with
Quiet violence.
Time dissolves and time creates.

*

Sometimes,
Intense heat can lead to cosy warmth
And not to a burning sensation.
Sometimes,
Sforzando can lead to piano;
Therefore,
Just be!

And one day, all my dreams were interrupted by the most wonderful reality!

(To my husband)

*

Gentle fairies -
7 beauties of the night -
Float on mist,
In a dance of furies.
Magic pot
That catches dew,
And pronounces all the chants,
Will untie the knot.
Lady's bedstraws
Are the link between their world
And this.
Be aware of the flaw.

(Romanian witchcraft)

Do not rewind,
Do not fast forward -
The same song sounds different each time you play it.
Shush and dance.

*

There is a Sun flake melting on your heart.

(June)

*

My sensation of your perception
Is one step away from
The duration
With which one offers
A certain suggestion
And then, regrets
Causing such indiscretion
And plastic expression
Of a lifetime indigestion.

15

It must be that the Moon imprisoned our summer.
Look at it shine tonight and
Almost whispering:
"The warmth is all mine!"

*

Faith should be practised with fine discretion only.

*

The whole of March
Was one big flood of
Melancholy and aching for the sunshine.
The ark we had to keep our spirits dry
Was made of films and books and music and long
chats.

You want my poem
To absolve you of the mundane.
I want my poem
To absorb you.

And what then?
It is your voice or
My thoughts,
That manipulate the pen?

*

Human, you are the breeze of imagination;
A fleeting essence confined within its shell,
As you sculpt it from within,
To preserve the divine and keep it apart from hell.

My yoga

An hour spent bathing in solitude,
And it feels like 100 years of perfect human silence.
You stretch your soul on white sheets of silence,
And the feet of your subconscious gently touch
The crips witness of this moment.

*

My thoughts landed on the shelf,
Just beneath the window,
Where a sun beam had been sleeping for a few good
hours.
Thoughts sat neatly, next to each other,
Without having to acknowledge one another.
Separation - meditation - sun salutation.

Ah, that stillness that arouses the poetry of deep observation.

*

We are constantly told to find silence and stillness and yet,
Nature is not silent, nature is not still.
The noise inside our bodies is as loud as life around us really is:
Constant movement, rhythm and connection -
That's how nature thrives,
That's how we came to be.
Our lips may be sealed at times,
But everything within us never quiets.
Take a pause to take that in -
That is your silence.

Your body -
This beautiful messy home
Of so much
That is still unknown.

The tenderness of this line of death,
The sharpness of this line of life -
There is so much colour in between the two!
Alone and anew -
I feel that I can reach the edge of
Today without having to go through.
I am relentless as of today!
I am to dream and sweat my thoughts on this
keyboard.
I am to write and find you and me,
And them all and the truth!

*

There is water running through the fabric of the living;
It is the memory of the first poem;
It is the dusk that flows amongst us.

They say -
As water meanders through,
It dissolves the limestone's hold.
Subtle transformations occur -
Unseen, untimely -
Crafting intricate caves.
They say -
As prayers traverse the world,
They dissolve darkness and the unknown;
They give rise to a faith that survives
The unseen and untimely,
Harmless and encoded
In visions and whispers.

*

Windows steaming dreams of last night -
It's like a crying of the awake.
I want to hug the floor,
But the sheets decide to enslave me for a minute more.
Oh lazy winter mornings!

Words are crowding in my mouth
In a celebratory temptation to sing,
To scream, to give my speech!
Who will even listen?
"I'll listen!" - the floor squeaks.
"Hear out: the windows cry no more."
It's day now, not just morning anymore.
It's December in the sky,
On Earth and in my soul.

*

December -
The heart is idle NOT in winter time,
When bodies get so cold
As if the chill refreshes all the bones and
Awakens YOU!
And makes you wander at every beam of sunlight.
There is no rhythm,
Unless you play one with your heart;
And there you have it -
You can be idle not
In winter time.

I wonder if the deceivingly peaceful savana that stretches ahead is a mirage or I am one. My heart is illiterate as it probably was in the moment of creation. The only feeling that evolves inside me is a longing, a deep nostalgia. For the first time, I wish I knew how to knit so that I could lay this golden warm late morning on a piece of cotton cloth and wrapt it around my heart and my body. Dots of time and question marks, that is what we, humans are.

(South Africa)

*

You cannot observe something that you are not part of. You are part of everything and everything is within you, therefore: Observe.

The illusion of this foggy Friday is
That life is just an app today but
There is no swiping back from the chores
Made or not made.
Word play tires the soul,
Yet here I am - doing so,
In this favourite room -
Lights dimmed,
Walls tiled with my dreams.
The puzzle has no exact pattern,
Not today anyway,
Not this one.
Fog is an escape of faults -
It's better we don't see through it.

October is a lagoon of leafs and wind.
The grapes taste sweeter,
The wine makes hearts softer.
There are passionate calls and text messages,
From lover over to another -
Invitations to hide from the incoming cold,
To glue their bodies under cover.
Clay of love will hold them tangled,
Aroma of whispers shall feed their souls;
They'll pray to those stars that reached a new dimension,
They will speak of hope.
Autumn is a laboratory of life.

*

Today, I cried good bye to this October -
My purest friend this year -
With all its winds and warmth of colours.
Good bye I say!
Come now winter,
You symphony of grey!

A sudden thought -
Unmade spirit of
Infinite number of Suns
That shine and set
Upon unclaimed memories
Of green meadows and
Inviting peaks of mountains
That speak through winds
Of here and far.
Oh sweet taste of Earth
And Life,
Do come!

*

We made reality redundant.

Here comes the fear -
A sweaty shadow dripping on the stained floor -
It makes no sound,
And brings a chilly glow
To every nightmare dancing on the wall.

*

I am seeing people for the first time,
And it feels like I have seen them before.
Am I sleep walking?
Am I dreaming of them all?
How do I take control?

*

We are all one collective dream that does not want to
end.

Oh, how eloquent a broken heart can be!

*

There are days when walking in my shoes feels strange
- as if I have erased the memory of who I was and who
I have been evolving into, in the past 5 years.

*

The morning fog has stabbed the heavy clouds and
now,
The Sun is healing souls and shinning roads.
November is a season in its own.

Dear November,
My vision melts in this marmalade of autumnal glow.

*

Sadness is a poet's must have accessory.
Poetry comes from darkness and travels towards the
light of a white piece of paper -
Another prison, an exhibition cage.

*

How can we make it up to all the great books that we
will never read?

Life is an endless improvisation of heaven and hell.

*

Rain is the most beautiful unwritten essay.

*

My bed is floating like a mirror in between worlds, and
I can see a large stone putting an end to every sentence
-
It is the Moon.
It carries messages between the after midnight
dreamers -
A dense network of questions mixed with emotions.
The dreamers risk never going back to reality;
They risk becoming prisoners in other peoples dreams;
They risk remaining nothing but messengers of the
moonlight.

Only the dead become immortals -
Until the living die and take their place.
Souls are sewn onto a map of memories that
Blend with nature;
They become an intertwining of concepts,
A process of understanding and accepting death.

*

For some, the sky is nothing but a concrete ceiling.

Pullover me -
I am warm,
I feel soft
And I lay calm.
I breathe hot,
While whispering fabrics of love
To turn creamy at night,
Dripping sensations of lust.
I am bluish in the daylight,32
Touch me!
I will turn bright.
Pullover me love,
And hold me tight.

Paint my hands on your face,
Paint your smile on my heart,
Paint the clouds in my hair,
Paint the rain in our loving stare.
Paint your memories on my pillow;
Paint my whispers on your window.
Paint this poem on our wall,
Paint our love and hear its call.

An age of mystery within a drop of rain.

*

God always comes when you are doing little things.

*

Rain is just another form of silence.

The rain is pouring down
As if the sky has broken
And the outer space is liquid.
Thoughts are now swimming,
Free of borders;
They are masters of the horizon,
Building rainbows.
Have I told you that
Today, it's raining?

*

I gaze and gaze into the sky -
This sea with many unseen ports,
Where I wish a ship carried me at ease and chance.
Its cloudy waves are gentle and forgiving -
In fact they are the heaven.

And one day, they brought the sky to us.
Its curved line touched our foreheads and our thoughts
dipped in confusion.
But how sweet the confusion!
That day, the sky was here, with us.
We bowed to it, we really did.

*

This day dream weather
Arrests my mind and thoughts
Without a caution,
Without the use of handcuffs.
Expelled from an environment,
I, universe within the Universe,
Swing open all the doors -
Those to the past,
And those to the future -
And memories and hopes intertwine,
To allow meditation upon a mortal's life.

The trees,
They've all just fallen from the sky
In ways no poem can describe -
just music maybe,
But it would be a composer's ninth.

The trees
Tremble in their static ritual,
While winds hum hallelujah,
And spread the virus of melancolia -
Oh poetry! Words are drunken with nostalgia.

*

Autumn is the mathematics of time.

*

The symphony of chestnut trees is music for the lonely.

Poetry,
The magic touch of understanding,
The spoken ritual of love.

*

I've written wonders
In secret thoughts of mine.
The ink was old though,
And here it is -
Forgetfulness aching me once more.

*

The spirit of a broken window
Hovers in the sky.
This silence is a lullaby
That put the past to restful sleep.
Good night!

I pickle Sun beams,
In jars of autumn melancholia,
To sprinkle them in winter time,
On my dreams of heavenly peperomia.

This silly weather
Makes me clouded with emotions and overwhelmed
With the theatre of nature -
Endless script of life and death.

*

Like a gentle whisper, the autumnal Sun creeps into
our late summer dream.

Autumn is the eternal return -
The womb awaits to hear the calling of your cry.
Retrace, remember, relive, resurrect
Each time.

*

Love futilely!
Live similarly to the flight of a butterfly!
The small and harmless will not be bothered
By norms and judgment.

I, Poems

I shiver!
Emotions lie drawn on my pillow.
Today is courageous as any other beginning.
And yet, here I am shivering.
January day dreams float in mist,
And fears are loud within me,
Like cawing crows that scare us
Because we do not understand that
They might just be looking for a friend.

*

It is the light that carries the weight of life;
Darkness covers and hypnotises to forget.
I have always preferred the noise of a city
To censure the silence within my head-
Where long chapters are being written without my
consent.

I burn
Every hope that I have,
On the skin of my memory.
I melt every doubt that I have
And I pick up the remnants
And I mould them in tiny figurines -
Relics for the future hopefuls.

*

I am the centre
Of a whirlwind of hopes and joys,
Overtaking my own understanding of this force.
My hair is messy and I catch my breath -
And for a sweet change-
I taste the pleasure of happy certainties.

I am a tree with roots bound beneath the asphalt -
A prisoner of man made ground.

*

Some days are just one big broken heart.

*

And sometimes,
All that matters is the feeling that there is a mirror in
the ceiling,
And that there is no end to all your day dreaming.

We live as many lives as the love stories that we
survive.

*

Tuscany -
A slice of heaven that feels
Like a stellar caprice,
That fell upon the tuscan hills.
The breeze, the buzzing, the knocking
Are poems seen and heard,
Through episodes of whistling wind and yawning
herds
Of hearts that are lazy and content.
With our minds in a state of awe,
We laugh and eat and nap and cheer -
And remember that in tennis you do now draw.

There is no gene for fate - we cannot alter it; it will not mutate.

*

Every ending is a death

If I am dying,
The night is not a blunder but an answer.
I stare for hours at the golden light,
Flowing from the lamp that does not shine on me;
It accolades and shines onto the darkened pages of my mind,
To zoom into my fears of ending
As they emerged from the beginning.
What kind of child is worried about death?
The child within this grown woman,
Who types on darkened pages
And wonders if she's dying -
Bit by bit, every day into the night.

Do you see what I see?
Do you see poetry in every tree?
Nature is a beautiful free anthology.

*

There are so many silhouettes in the sky -
An orgy of shapes that answer to the question:
What is English winter rain?

*

The commotion that they had heard,
Turned out to be a fallen cloud
That found an empty tub in an abandoned backyard.
The cloud rained all its existence,
Filling the tub with a liquid
That murmured of the sky.

In a world of robots,
How would angels be?
With electric wings,
And empty of humanity;
Crying only with one sound,
Finding laughter non profound.
Would they be praying to a human?
Guarding upon their summon?
I question my robot,
I await to see
If my robot really wants to be.

*

The most difficult age is the age of doubt.

Voices and perfumes - the perfect reminders.

*

When Nothing separates itself into particles of something - that is when life happens.

*

It's when we are suspicious of our own actions that we are most uncomfortable in our own skin.

To my grandmother

A sorrowful regret sits on the armchair
Next to the terracotta stove -
It's me!
I can smell the terracotta as it warms up -
I can see the evil dance of the flames though the cracks
And I turn my eyes to to windows - frozen
From the cold outside.
You are still lying on the bed -
You are still dying -
You have punished me to only feel regret.
I miss you and I so wish I had come to see
Your lifeless body so that I can
Accept.

*

We all want to be loved with the intensity of a sinner's
first prayer.

She dreams of demons in the sky,
Of rainless days and endless nights -
Dreams of sweat mixing with stardust,
Of unheard words, ancient and robust.

Her sexuality confined, trapped in stone,
Motherhood lost, forever unknown.
Her love now digitalised, cold and stark,
Only a machine could truly embark.

Within her skin, a complex yearning resides,
The eternal quest to grasp and comprehend sin's tide -
Her sin, his sin, no one's or everyone's to blame,
Yet the possibility of finding none, still remains.

Yet she senses its presence as the Earth awakens,
The sin that lingers before the dawn breaks.
Only one sin reigns, both sacred and profane -
The sin of losing hope, the sin of choosing pain.

Friends are courage.

Evil cannot cloak itself within silence,
For it needs words laced with malice,
Chaos and screams of anguish,
It craves the flames that scorch,
And the bullets that kill.

Evil cannot take root in music,
It withers amidst the songs of birds,
The gentle cooing of cherished babies, and the laughter
of joyful souls.

Beware, evil is at large.

A delicate trace, akin to hand-sewn lace,
Patterns woven with no apparent place,
Yet enabling the departed to breathe,
Though their life force lies deep beneath;
They may be forgotten, or so it seems,
But their blood lingers on in unseen streams.

The baton is passed, generation to generation,
Youth don their armour, fuelled by determination,
Casting aside any hint of fear,
They tread the path of their predecessors, clear;
A path stained with blood, a recurring plight,
Yet they march on, ready to fight.

*

What if the very essence of stability is embodied in a
wave?

Amongst newly bathed verdant leaves,
Strawberries that grace a coffee cup,
And silence drapes in gentle pleats -
Within me, all things carry on,
Ever onward and forward;
Yet my hands somewhat clumsy and nervous,
Persist to type, to tidy, to applaud,
To clasp and then reach out
Yearning for your touch,
My dear.

*

I am a sanctuary of memories and experiences;
What tales my body holds!
What wonders my mind enfolds!
Oh September,
I offer you my gratitude for this indian summer's bliss,
A weeks's worth of wondrous poems, sheer and
endless.

Leave the dreaming to the born dreamers.

*

I have vivid memories of the gardens from my childhood. One was located in the house where I grew up, while the other belonged to my grandparents' country house. Both were magical Gardens of Eden like - spaces where all my dreams came to be, the beginning to everything and the end to a certain era all at the same time. I guess children who grow up in gardens are all blessed to have tasted from the fruits of innocence before reaching out to the forbidden.

With thoughts aligned behind
The heavy curtains of her smokey eyes,
The smile took lead,
And thus protected her that night.

*

It speaks in truths braided with nostalgia,
It is born under the zodiac of fallen stars,
And from the inception of a cosmic dream.
It takes away your disappointment,
And sighs in a rhythm meant to invite
immortality.
I present to you: poetry.

The night seemed to scorch the Moon's feet
As it descended too far and deep,
To taste the earthly balmy air - so sweet!
This morning, the silence reminds us
Of that moment in the summer past;
Of nights that do not burn but they
Cool in a chorus of thunders,
And a thriller of lightings.
August and September,
Under the sign of the twins
Have switched and play a game
That nobody wins, but us,
The mere mortals, for the time being.
The only gain is our present time -
Or so it feels.

Our bodies are bittersweet memories of how time travels through life.

*

"Clouds are growing old."
"But that has not happened in so long!"
"I know…"
Quiet… wind devastating life outside the heavy door.
"Life is nothing but a morning storm! We now know that we will have to face it for so long."

*

A long sigh is
The body's manner of
Signing out;
It is a nostalgic cry.

You.
Tiny dot seen from above
And yet so great down here,
On the ground.
You
Dreamed and conquered,
Created and developed
And now you're torn and drunken,
Very close to sunken.
What serpent has infected your ideas?
It doesn't really matter now -
Your time and hope are in arrears.

*

How often are you quiet enough
To listen to the whispers of your heart?

Have you ever felt your body being soothingly rocked by your heart?

*

Silence in daylight is a teaser by excellence.

*

When we think about its impact on mental health, social media is nothing but a slaughterhouse for spirits, with see through walls.

We can and we will regain our humanity and our right to be here, on this planet, when we will relearn to observe, to marvel at the world around us (both near and far), to have the patience to feel this world and not just journal about it.

*

Let nature silence you at times.

*

A poem, if not read out loud, just once - at least - it will vanish, it will be reabsorbed by the vastness of the blank paper it was typed on.

If I must be, let me be more forceful than the wind,
Uncaring and ruthless and blind to devastation.

I sometimes need to be without worrying of being too
much or too little.
I need not care whether I finish every sentence.

And you, if you started to explore,
You would find a fortress in each one of my words -
Letters standing like bespoke walls.

But you do not care,
And you do not really read -
You simply stare.

Miles of stones
Stained with footsteps
Of carriers of souls,
Of different faiths,
Or none at all,
Or empty shells.
Endless trails
Of clouds that cover up
The tales of this city,
That never fails.

*

Truth is immaterial.
Imagination, on the other hand,
Is a magic substance that we use
To intoxicate the living and the dead with.
Legends of the living
Are no stronger than
The legends of the dead.

The Moon -
Silent driver of the tides,
Photographer of our nights -
An island in the outer space,
Poetry that sounds like grace.

*

Creaky floorboards -
Cramps of time,
That only memories can alleviate,
Ever so slight - ly -
- rycs now no longer rhyme.
We are two pairs
Of beaten shoes
That match and fit,
And walk along the spine
Of all that is to come
With time.

Make your smile a magic clue;
Make your smile a timeless glue.

*

You are the music that I will listen to
When I am gone.
What haunting thought,
I know my love.
But when I will be a shadow,
A memory of who I am today -
From behind closed curtains,
From beyond this place,
From inside the world of ever after,
I shall be waiting to hear the music of your laughter.

The moon is an ancient care home for the dying dreams.

*

There is no sobering up from being a poet.

*

We are knitting time in meshes of quiet music of our hearts and faded memories that never fall apart. It's Saturday and summer feels a tad sad.

I swim in sunsets,
When dreams come flying,
Smelling darkness from afar.
They do not come from within,
They belong to demons and angels
Staring down, intently through the sky…
Night, night…

*

There is a moment of indescribable stillness just after the rain quiets down… it could be mystical if the city wasn't so profane.

Writing is the most strenuous exercise of patience.
Writers are anything but patient.

*

We burned and melted like oddly scented candles -
Such pain and pleasure.
The rain glossed over the waxy figurines
That now keep still in the breezeless after rain thrill.
(Summer heat)

*

Zoom into the zen
Of a rainy summer day - poet's den.

Our brains sometimes behave like a retired postman who finally delivers all that correspondence kept hidden in his sack. Waves of recollections start knocking at your door without an explanation. It is often the result of deep subconscious exploration.

*

Think of stillness as a muscle. Exercise it and you will then enjoy the fruits of a grateful mind.

I live on Earth - a tiny blue dot,
Where the sound of rain makes some kind of love
To the smell of after the rain.
I love my planet Earth,
Where life sprouts and grows and then evolves.
I am a creature of the Earth -
I dream of other planets and far away galaxies,
Only because life on Earth is an incubator for all
dreams.
I listened to the sound of blood pumping through my
heart once,
And all I could think of was that life on Earth pumps
Light through anything that's dark.

Winter - so dark!
And yet, we are all bright and
Try to be merry and light!
We activate invisible antennas
That function anywhere throughout our bodies,
Scanning for outer signals of snow.
The city is like Scrooge -
Does not believe that snow
Exists or ever was.
We send white envelopes
Containing glitter and merry wishes.
How deceitful!
Oh how we deceive one another!
But hold on, perhaps there is hope;
I suddenly feel sleepy and low -
The antenna seems to say that
This winter, there are chances of snow!

A ripe peach with cracked skin - that's what a loving
heart would look like on my canvas if I was a painter.

*

Candle wax resembles death's sweat,
Hardening swiftly with impending threat.
Rain washes it away,
Clouds tie knots in the sky's gray.

The gates of Heaven remain closed,
Earth seems naught but a maze exposed.
Remember, oh do remember,
The sadness of this bloody November.

The world is burning
And yet, my feet are terribly cold -
Treading through the mud of dark
Ominous shadows that clack,
And whisper rather than talk.
They finally voice
The foretold mission that they have;
I warm my feet up and my ears
Start burning in distress
At knowing that the effect
This mission will have,
Is absolute regress.
I stress and constantly press
My head on the pillow,
To sweat off the knowledge.
I know it's to no avail.
Human darkness will
Very likely and unfortunately prevail.

Earth, a sacred temple in this vast Universe.
What have we done, failing as its entrusted priests?
Why have we desecrated its sanctity, trashing its beauty?
Silence! Let us cease our noise, humans!
Pause our actions, halt our reactions, if only momentarily.
Let us take a moment of complete silence.

*

"I am sorry" someone sings in the blue garden.
Beneath the towering tea tree, a blind dog finds solace.
The wind dances, ensnared in the tree's leaves.
The melody of sorries and sorrow flows
Akin to the darkness of the Cosmos -
Just as it was before the birth of Word.
A moment of chaos emerges -
Suddenly, a bomb detonates in some distant place,
Extinguishing the song into a blaze of silence.
The memory of the last day before the terror
Fades away, replaced by
A brand new world that emerges with the dawn.

Exhaustion seeps from the worn armchair of an elderly
man.
His cane is trapped in the decaying, old floor.
An ancient melody fills his ears,
Marching to accompany him.
The man's eyelids concede defeat.
His body surrenders to rest,
As his soul bathes in the gentle moonlight.

*

Loving will always give you more strength than being
loved!

*

Streets are soaked with remnants of last night;
The cars are driving at a lazy pace
To allow the noise of people who talk,
Dogs that bark, a coffee machine's steam
And clank.
It's a Sunday in London,
And I am back.

The Ghost of faith
Roams within this city of the old,
Which cannot give itself entirely to the new.
The walls of all the churches that they erected
Are the very flesh of the mighty Ghost of faith itself -
A breathing memory,
That crosses again and again,
In its endless loving way.
A child is the beginning and the end,
And beams light through the clear of windows
That are never to be painted or tainted,
As it was by Wren ordained.

*

A woman's eyes, twenty thousands leagues under the
sea of life.

I am pathologically romantic.

*

You cannot go far without the magic.

*

I clamber into each day;
My heart pumps softly,
My joints are numb.
I memorise the pillow,
And I grab the floor with my feet.
Spreading my toes,
I put my hands together into prayer,
And here I go! (Pain)

I dance beneath the Moon's glow,
To the rhythm of Rachmaninoff's flow,
That starts its session in the rusty fall.
The light suddenly yearns for sound,
Uniting all spirits that abound.
What overture of flying creatures,
That resist the take off,
Enraptured by the dawn's light.
The words are overwhelmingly romantic,
Crafting very odd semantics.
There will be time to study it all -
Because you see, time is on the slow -
It is autumn and inner life will freely flow.

She drank the water to drown the butterflies.

*

What happens to all the memories carved out of me?
Are they vacuumed into a void or are they existing
independently? Do they have a destiny outside mine?

*

Our skin is made of sun and wind and holds against us
so much sin.

And now, the light depends on me,
Perspective transformed into art, you see.
I blue myself into reality,
And I yearn to yellow into the sunset.

I leap into the space where
There is trust between myself and my ideas.
Time has no place in here.
I do not judge, or at least I try.

The gate to jump back,
Slides shut.
I blue red myself to sleep,
The colours fade and I am scared to dream.

My body is the sacred space now,
And it is so warm and familiar;
A blend of data and of hormones;
It feels lovely to be me.

Some people direct smiles at you that go straight into your heart. Take care of these patches of warmth - they are a great first aid kit for your soul.

*

There is poetry in between your body and your soul.

The (Never)End

.

Printed in Great Britain
by Amazon

34789460R00047